ABCs

OF YOUR SUCCESS

WRITTEN BY JOYCE BENNETT

DESIGNED BY WENDY BYLE

ABCs

OF YOUR SUCCESS

www.ABCsofLiving.com

Written by Joyce Bennett

Designed by Wendy Byle

Published by

ACORN PRESS

Printed in U.S.A.

INTRODUCTION

Are there things in your life that you would like to change, or add? Do you have some goals or dreams you would like to realize in the next week, month or year? Have you given thanks for all the wonderful things that have happened to you each day, last month or last year? Have you worked through any anger or frustration that might have come about due to the "not so wonderful things" that might have happened in your life during the past year or years? How about your relationships with your family and friends? Have they deepened or do your relationships with them need more work?

There are books, magazines, lectures, and various other self-improvement modalities that are helpful in answering these questions. Different religions and spiritual philosophies also have road maps on how to live life, which are contained in their particular creed, dogma or sacred writing. However, in some cases, these writings are complex and convoluted. Using *ABCs of Your Success* is simple and can ultimately help in realizing goals or dreams.

Every year some of my friends and I visit a boarding school on a Native American Indian reservation in Northern Arizona. While visiting one of the teacher's homes, I noticed that there was a piece of paper taped to her bathroom wall. Upon closer inspection, it was an inspirational outline using the alphabet as a guideline on how to live life. As I read these twenty-six sentences, I knew intellectually everything I was reading, however, it was a reminder to me—sort of a spiritual nudge, if you will—to take a look at how I had been living my life. It also rang true in my heart that this really is a simple road on how to live life and to realize goals and dreams. After reflecting on my life and these alphabetical sentences I expanded them to short chapters. I would like to share them with you and hope they will inspire you to do some reflecting as well.

CONTENTS

AVOID

A

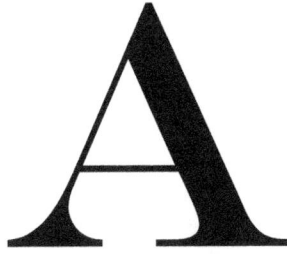

AVOID NEGATIVE PEOPLE, PLACES AND THINGS

Negative people rob us of our energy. It takes a lot of energy to live life. Have you ever felt drained after being with a negative person? Someone who complains about anything and everything? That person is zapping your energy! Avoid these people if possible. If they are family members and you cannot or don't want to avoid them, just listen. Don't get caught up in their negative drama. Have shorter visits with them. Give yourself permission. Think of another A—Advocate. Be your own advocate and protect yourself from these "energy vampires."

Stay away from negative places that bring up bad memories or are dangerous. Like negative people, places can drain us of our energy and block us from tapping into our creative source.

Avoid negative habits like excessive drinking, smoking, overeating or overspending. Get rid of them any way you can. These habits block your creativity. There are all kinds of resources to help us rid ourselves of negative habits.

Last but not least, avoid negative thinking. Stop criticizing yourself; it is self-defeating. It is okay to tell yourself that you are great for you *are* great. Your creator creates only greatness of which we are a part. Avoid criticizing and judging other people. Everyone has a story and a path to follow. We are not here to tell other people how to live their lives, or what path to follow. We are here to create our own story by following a path leading us to become the best we can be. Live your life in greatness.

Avoid these negative sources, and you'll be on your way to success.

AVOID NEGATIVE PEOPLE, PLACES AND THINGS

Suggested Exercises

- Think of some people in your life that may rob you of your energy—people who are complainers, who always see the glass half empty or who are just plain negative. Make a list of these people and then review it.

- Think of some places that may bring up negative feelings or are possibly dangerous to you physically or mentally. Make a list of these places and then review it.

- If you have habits that you think are negative and are blocking your creativity, write them down and then review your list.

- List some of the ways you criticize yourself. At the end of the list write down some things about yourself that are great.

BELIEVE

B

BELIEVE IN YOURSELF

Sometimes we don't feel very motivated. We feel like we are out of fuel. We start having self-defeating thoughts. Seeing ourselves as failures is easier than visualizing success. We define ourselves by our self-defeating thoughts or images of ourselves.

"I am not good enough." "I am just not smart enough." "I am too fat." or "I am too short." We may blame others for our misgivings, or for not reaching our goals. We may blame instead of believing. Blame is giving your power away—believing in yourself increases your power.

We already know how to achieve our goals. We may not know the details but we have the overall big picture. Believe in yourself and the details will fill in. You possess the power to accomplish anything you want. Define yourself by your inner qualities. What you believe about yourself and life becomes true for you. Believe in yourself. We are part of an amazing tapestry called life. This tapestry is woven with many different designs and colors. Each design is unique and brilliant.

This tapestry would be less rich and less beautiful without your being a part of it. Just knowing that we are part of something so much greater than ourselves gives us the power to create and accomplish anything we set out to do. This power is the fuel that motivates us to reach our goals. Believing we are so much more is the key to the vault that holds our dreams and the secret to our success.

We all have strengths and weaknesses; however, we all have the power to overcome our weaknesses and capitalize on our strengths. It is the dwelling-on our negative self-image that keeps us from reaching our goals or manifesting our dreams. What we think of ourselves will shape our destiny. Our self-image determines our choices, shapes our belief systems, and really takes over our life. Our self-image becomes our self-fulfilling prophecy.

Believe in yourself and your unique design and color in this tapestry of life. Let the details fall into place. Never stop believing in yourself; you are the one and only you. You are great; the greatest! You are a perfect piece of art and an important piece of the tapestry. Believe that and all things are possible. If you believe in God, a higher power, or something greater than yourself, then ask, "Would my creator create anything less than perfect?" The answer is "no."

We all know the carnival ride called "Bumper Cars." The object of the ride is to bump into as many cars as you can to get them out of your way. Sometimes we drive our vehicle like that. We bump into obstacles that keep us from reaching our goals. We are in the driver's seat of our vehicle we use to get around in life.

If we believe in ourselves, we will be able to navigate around those obstacles that appear before us on the road to our goals. When we see ourselves as accomplishing anything we wish, the power in the universe supports us, guides us and propels us toward reaching our goals and dreams. There is an eternal creative force within us just waiting to be tapped and channeled into wonderful, joyful creativity. Creative energy can be seen in science, art, literature, and relationships in a positive way. We will not only reach our goals and dreams, we can begin making a difference in the world. Believe in yourself. You are truly wonderful. Be full of wonder and you *will fulf*ill your dreams!

BELIEVE IN YOURSELF

Suggested Exercises

- Since a belief is nothing more than a feeling of absolute certainty about what something means, our beliefs therefore can help us reach our goals, or can hinder us. They can be unconscious or conscious, and they often stem from things we've heard or seen, felt a lot of emotion about, and then repeated to ourselves again and again until we felt certain. Write down all the old beliefs that have kept you from following through on your goal(s) in the past.

- Make a list of *new beliefs* that will empower you from this day forward.

CONSIDER
ALL ANGLES

C

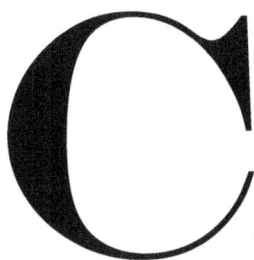

CONSIDER YOUR GOALS AND DREAMS
FROM ALL ANGLES

Goals or dreams change from time to time. Sometimes they change while on the path to realizing our goal or dream, or they may change at the moment we realize our goal or dream. However, each time we set a new goal, consider things from every angle. We must consider things from the heart as well as intellectually.

We may ask the question, "Does this goal or dream express all aspects of who I am? Does it embody all that I am spiritually, mentally, emotionally and physically?" This is a very important question because if it doesn't, you may fail in achieving your goal or manifesting your dream. You could end up following a dream or reaching for a goal that does not support your highest good.

Our lives consist of four aspects: Spiritual, mental, emotional and physical. The spiritual level provides a foundation for the development of other levels. Make sure your goals are in alignment with your universal life source, your oneness with life, and they will support your highest good.

Your mind holds all of your beliefs and values. Ask yourself, "Am I conscious of my thought patterns? Do I have a clear understanding of my belief system? Do my beliefs, values and philosophies support my highest good?" If you become aware of any beliefs, values or philosophies that fall short, you may want to do some work on this level before considering the next.

Since our ability to relate to another and the world on a feeling level comes from our emotional level, we want to be aware of what and how we feel at any given time. Am I fulfilled in my relationship with myself and others? If you are not aware, or not fulfilled, you may need to do some emotional healing work before continuing on your journey to realize your goal or dream.

The final aspect to consider is our physical bodies. They include our ability to survive and thrive in this world.

"Have I developed the skills to live comfortably and effectively in the world?" "Am I in tune with my body?" "Do I listen to what my body is telling me?" Our bodies know what they need. They communicate clearly and specifically, if we listen. "Am I understanding and interpreting my body's signals correctly?"

If we are aligned spiritually, have a clear understanding of our values and beliefs, have a good relationship with ourselves and others, and understand our physical needs, we're ready for our journey to success!

CONSIDER YOUR GOALS AND DREAMS FROM ALL ANGLES

Suggested Exercises

- List some of the goals you want to reach.

- Review the list. Do they support you spiritually? Do they support your highest good? Are they in alignment with your chosen spiritual path?

- Review your goal list *again*. Do they support you mentally? Do they support your beliefs and values?

- Review your goal list *one more time*. Do they support you emotionally? Do your goals assist you or block you from being aware of what you feel at any given time? Do they support you or keep you from being fulfilled in your relationship with yourself and others?

- Review your goal list a *final time*. Do your goals support you physically? Since your ability to survive and thrive in the world depends on the skills you acquire, do your goals assist and support you with developing these skills? Are your goals in alignment with your physical health or your financial security?

- Revisit any goals that don't support all four of these areas: spiritually, mentally, emotionally and physically.

DON'T GIVE UP

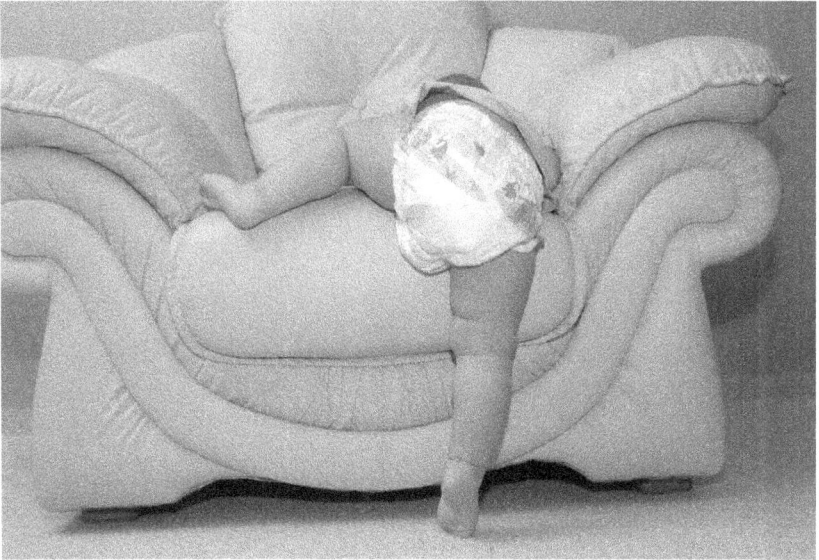

D

DON'T GIVE UP AND DARE TO SUCCEED

We all want to reach our goals and manifest our dreams, yet some people reach them and some don't. Why is that? Why aren't we all what we want to be? Well, we all have a list of excuses and use them as reasons why we are not successful or living our dream. The "A" section of this book talks about how negative self-talk is self-defeating. Negative self-talk translates into why we are not living up to our full potential. Go through your list of self-defeating excuses as to why you fall short of your goals.

"I don't have the education," or "I'm bald," or "I am too old" may sound familiar. These are *excuses* not reasons. We fear setting goals. What if we don't make it? What if we fail? We will be embarrassed! Fear is what stops us all!

We can have anything we want if we tell ourselves what we want and direct our conscious minds to reach for it. Once we do that, the subconscious mind will take over and figure out the details.

There was a man who was born in 1809 in a log cabin in Kentucky. His parents were born in Virginia, of undistinguished families. When he was 7 years old, his family moved to Indiana, where both his younger brother and his mother died shortly thereafter. Several years later, his older sister died in childbirth. He moved to Illinois in 1830 and worked several jobs, including surveying, serving as postmaster, a shopkeeper, and made an unsuccessful run for the Illinois legislature in 1832.

The store went out of business. He purchased another store with a partner. This venture ultimately failed, leaving him badly in debt. Two years later, his former partner died, increasing his debt. That very same year, the lady he loved died from fever.

This man married in 1842, the union produced four children. Only one reached adulthood. The man had many political setbacks before he was ultimately elected as the 16th U.S. President. His name was Abraham Lincoln.

After Lincoln's election, many Southern states, fearing Republican abolition of slavery, seceded from the Union. Lincoln faced the greatest internal crisis of any U.S. President. After the fall of Fort Sumter, Lincoln raised an army and fought to save the Union from falling apart. Initially, Lincoln anticipated a short conflict; he called for 75,000 volunteers to serve three months. Despite enormous pressures, loss of life, battlefield setbacks, poor generals and assassination threats, Lincoln stuck with this pro-Union policy for four long years of civil war. On January 1, 1863, the Emancipation Proclamation declared freedom for all slaves in the Confederacy. Lincoln never gave up!

Abraham Lincoln is remembered for his vital role in preserving the Union during the Civil War and ending slavery in the United States. He is also remembered for his character, as a man of humble origins whose determination and perseverance led him to the nation's highest office.

Don't give up, no matter what. Dare to succeed!

DON'T GIVE UP AND
DARE TO SUCCEED

Suggested Exercises

- Write down some things you have given up on in the past.

- Write down why you think you gave up.

- What fears are in the way of you succeeding in reaching your goal(s)?

- Finally, write down some things that you have accomplished, achieved or done successfully in your life. Congratulate yourself for what you have achieved and use your successes to inspire you toward your goal(s).

ENTHUSIASM

E

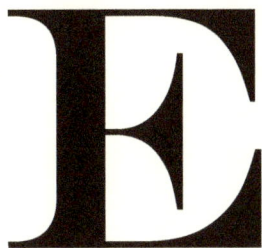

ENTHUSIASM MATTERS

Enthusiasm means "one with the energy of God." It derives from root words relating to being inspired and possessed by the Divine. There is something awesome about people practicing this spiritual quality. They are vibrantly alive.

In the book, *Spiritual Literacy,* author Mary Ann Brussat includes a story written by Margret M. Stevens about three brick masons who are busy at work. When the first is asked what he is building, he answers without looking up, "I'm laying bricks." The second replies, "I'm building a wall." But the third responds with great enthusiasm, "I am building a cathedral." Enthusiasm lights up your life and the lives of those around you.

In an essay, newspaper columnist Linda Weltner wrote, "Modern life can grow dull and predictable... still there's one magic talisman left that has the power to bring freshness, novelty and surprise into your life. Someone else's enthusiasm." Again, look at the meaning of the word, this time through scientist Louis Pasteur: "The Greeks have given us one of the most beautiful words of our language, the word enthusiasm—a God within. The grandeur of the acts of men is measured by the inspiration from which they spring. Happy is he who bears a God within."

Each and every one of us is exactly where we are in life according to the consciousness we hold. So if you don't like where you are in your life, or your goals seem unattainable, then, you must find your consciousness. Our consciousness is the root of our enthusiasm. Become enthusiastic about life, and you will enjoy all of life's riches. Enthusiasm is what propels us forward on our path toward our goals.

There are other "E" words we can incorporate into our way of living. Excitement—be excited about life itself. Be excited about your goals. Excitement leads to enthusiasm. Taking the journey enthusiastically shortens the road to your goals.

Another "E" word is "Entitlement".

Do you believe you are entitled to your dreams, your goals, or abundant living? Do you believe the Divine Presence, or God, as you understand God to be, is all around you as a fish lives in water? If so, can the fish of the sea ever lack for water? Can we be in the sea of divine presence or the energy of God, and ever lack a sufficient amount of creativity, ideas, money or opportunities in our time of need? The answer is no. You must believe that you are entitled to your goals and dreams, get excited about them, and take your journey with enthusiasm. If you do, your success is guaranteed!

ENTHUSIASM MATTERS

Suggested Exercises

- How enthusiastic are you about your life? List some things about your life that you are enthusiastic about.

- List some things that you are not enthusiastic about.

- How can you change the things about your life that you are not enthusiastic about? Write them down.

- There is another E you might want to consider. Take a look at your spiritual *economics*. List your views on affluence. Prosperity in the broadest sense can mean "spiritual well-being" or "healthy spiritual economics." Upon reviewing your list, do you have the consciousness to attract the things you want in your life? If not, what changes could you make in your thinking that would increase your spiritual well-being?

FAMILY

F

FAMILY AND FRIENDS ARE TREASURES, SEEK OUT THEIR RICHES

Families come in all shapes and forms. Some consist of a mother and father, some have just one parent and some have a grandparent or guardian. No matter how your family looks, seek out the riches of their treasures. They will assist you on your journey in reaching your goals.

Even though family encouragement and inspiration are obvious riches, there are hidden treasures in the challenges we may face with our families. These challenges help you grow spiritually and emotionally. The more you grow and become aware of your own power, the easier reaching your goals and dreams become.

You also have another family—the human family. Each person in this family has a gift for you. Take the time to find it.

I want to share a story with you about a flight I took to Phoenix, Arizona. There was a young man with Downs syndrome sitting in the middle with his caretaker in the window seat. It was obvious that people had walked by avoiding the aisle seat next to him. So I decided to sit and appreciate being near the front of the plane. Well, this young man offered me the most delightful gift of being a new friend. He told me his name and it was quite obvious he was nervous about the takeoff. We chatted and by the time we started to taxi, we had become fast friends. I asked him if he would like to hold hands during takeoff. He said "yes," so we did. We sat holding hands for quite a while after takeoff and continued to talk with the help of his caretaker, as he had trouble articulating words. He told me his mom and sister died and he was going to live with his cousin. He told me about his dog and how he liked having his pretzels in the evening. How he liked to take his shower, get into his pajamas, and watch television before he went to bed. Even though he was difficult to understand verbally, I understood what his heart was saying. I felt connected to it. Sadness came over me when we started to land. I knew my new friend and I would part soon. As we walked through the terminal, we waved goodbye and went our separate ways. He will live in my heart always.

Each person we meet is part of our human family. They bring us gifts. Accept them, for they will enrich your life and assist you on your journey to reach your goals. Determining what that gift means is up to you. It may not take the form you expect.

FAMILY AND FRIENDS ARE TREASURES, SEEK OUT THEIR RICHES

Suggested Exercises

- Make a list of your immediate family. What "riches" do they offer you? Write them down next to each name.

- Make a list of your extended family. What "riches" do they offer you? Write them down next to each name.

- Make a list of some of your close friends. What "riches" do they offer you? Write them down next to each name.

- Make a list of other friends and acquaintances in your life. What "riches" do they offer you?

GIVE

G

GIVE MORE THAN YOU PLANNED

The ABCs. How simple life is really. Life isn't out to "get" anyone of us. Life doesn't favor anyone of us. Life just happens. Life doesn't pick and choose whose dreams or goals will be realized. Life is how we view it. It is a perceptual experience. Perceive it as perfect and it is perfect. How we experience life — how we perceive life — is in direct relation to what we give in life.

Giving and receiving are two sides of the same coin. To complete a gift, there must be a giver who truly wants to give and a receiver who wants to receive. The giver creates a vacuum after giving and is now ready to receive; the recipient is in a position to give. The receiver need not give something back to the same person. Both giver and receiver keep the flow of giving and receiving going and allows everything to move freely in and out of their lives. Holding on to anything blocks the flow like the ebb and flow of the tides in the ocean. It is a cycle.

Visualize a circle of people with each person giving to and receiving from another person in the circle. If one person holds on too long, the flow stops and everyone in the circle feels the block in energy. When everything moves freely around the room, everyone receives the benefits as well as the energy, which circulates also.

Earlier, we talked about family. We are all part of this human family. We are in relationships of different types in this human family. If we don't get what we want in our relationships, we need to look at what we give. Giving is an important part of receiving. The way we give to others is the way the universe will give to us. Giving money, things, or love is truly a gift to yourself. It creates a circulation of energy in your life. The more energy circulating, the wealthier you are in all aspects of life.

If more money is a goal, give money. If a new job is a goal, what do you give to your current job?

Giving affirms abundance and helps us feel prosperous. If we wrap our hands around money, our hands are not open to receive more.

Giving has a partner: Gratitude. When we feel grateful, we are in a state of happiness. We are kinder, more generous, and friendlier. This behavior makes your life better automatically and helps you to live your life more fully.

Time seems to collapse as we attain our goals since people whom reflect your thoughts, feelings and experiences seem to be drawn to you. Gratitude reflects back to us in wonderful ways. In the Eastern philosophy it is known as Karma, the currency of your life. With Karma, we purchase and create our life experiences: Good, bad, pleasant or unpleasant.

Give more than you planned. Whether it be love, money, time, kindness or friendship. Give more than you planned to give. Give without expectations. Give without condition—then give more—then give even more. Remember to be grateful for what you have.

GIVE MORE THAN YOU PLANNED

Suggested Exercises

- Write down what percentage of your financial income you are tithing?

- Do you tithe some of your time by volunteering? If not, make a list of places you could do some volunteer work.

- Create a daily Gratefulness Journal and write down five things you are grateful for each day.

HANG ON

H

HANG ON TO YOUR GOALS AND DREAMS

Hang on to your goals and dreams no matter what. Remember the poster of a cat hanging by his paws from a tree branch with the caption, "Hang in there?" There are times when my goals and dreams seem so far away; however, I remember that poor cat every time I feel discouraged. I hang in there, even though it feels like I hang on by my fingernails.

Obstacles get in our way, on the road to our dreams. We may feel like we can't move them. Well, if we can't move them, we go around. We waste precious time and energy trying to move the unmoveable.

I once met a man who wanted to become a marathon runner. This was his dream. There were major challenges facing him when he got older. However, he clung to his dream. He practiced under some grueling circumstances. Even though the pain was almost unbearable, he continued to train. It took him several years to become conditioned enough to participate in a marathon. He took his place at the starting line. Although he came in last, he did finish the race. As he crossed the finish line the spectators as well as the other participants cheered him on. You see, he had no feet. Can you imagine the obstacles he had to overcome to reach his dream? He overcame them because he hung on to his dream. Hang on to yours!

HANG ON TO YOUR GOALS AND DREAMS

Suggested Exercises

- Review letters A, B, D and E. Then ask yourself these questions.

- Are you avoiding people that don't support your goals or dreams?

- Are you believing in yourself?

- Are you daring to succeed?

- Are you excited about your goals?

- If the answer to any of these questions is "no", then I would suggest rereading the chapter that applies. Keep applying the principles addressed in these chapters to encourage you to "hang on to your goals and dreams."

IGNORE

I

IGNORE THE OPINIONS OF OTHERS

Why share your goals with people who say things like, "Why would you want to do that?"

Have you ever said, "Boy I have a great idea," shared it, and had someone give his or her negative opinion about it? Do you remember how you felt? Did you feel empowered? Did you feel as enthused about your idea after hearing their negative opinion? Of course not. We give our power away if we listen to negativity. Life will not be as rich. Goals and dreams may never come to fruition. Success will elude us.

Our obsessive need for acceptance and approval from other people hinders us from realizing our goals. This "need" permeates all areas of our lives, our relationships at home and at work. It affects how we spend our money, the way we dress, the way we respond to both loved ones and strangers alike. It can even affect the kind of food we eat and what time we get up in the morning. The need to please other people causes us to have unsatisfying life-styles and remain in unsupportive relationships. Carried to the extreme, this need to please others can cause illness, poverty, and even death.

If we run our lives based on what other people think of us, we destroy our own self-creativity, our essence. If we live our lives to please others, we chip away at ourselves. If we focus our energies on pleasing other people, allow the opinions of others to matter, our lives will be less than magnificent. If we live to please, our lives will be one of constant confusion and dissatisfaction.

When I say, "Ignore the opinion of others," I do not mean, "Don't listen to anything." Refusing to listen, closes the door on opportunities to learn. Use what people think of you or your ideas as a guide for your life. Our reflection on what someone else says about us gives a clearer view of ourselves and allows personal growth. Avoid using the input from others to feel guilty, wrong, or insecure. When we *change* to please others, the vicious circle begins.

We can either take the view of another and use it to reinforce negative mental patterns we may have already or we can use the information to get rid of that which we do not want. Choosing the latter gives us opportunity for growth in every area of our lives. Growing and improving is the foundation for our success.

Avoid listening to the voice of fear. We hear it in other people's negative opinions. Listen to your own inner voice of courage. That voice will keep you moving on the path to success.

IGNORE THE OPINIONS OF OTHERS

Suggested Exercises

- Write down the things you <u>don't do</u> because you're afraid of "what other people might think."

- Write down the things you <u>do</u> that you don't want to do, but continue doing because you're afraid of "what other people might think."

- Review both lists and reflect on what you wrote down.

- Now, go out and do those things you have been afraid to do and *stop doing what you don't want to do*. Ignore the opinions of others!

JUST TAKE
ACTION

J

JUST TAKE ACTION!

Procrastination is your worse enemy when it comes to living life fully, reaching your goals and realizing your dreams. Reaching them requires action. We can dream, visualize, and write affirmations about meeting goals. Unless we take action, we will not realize them.

If you want to sing, get a voice coach and take lessons. If you want to be an attorney, go to school and study the law. Professional race car drivers, golfers or any other sports figure take the steps necessary to become what they are. They take action!

We may get stuck and not know what to do next. It actually doesn't matter what we do; just do something! We will get the energy moving around us. The stimulation of energy will guide us.

Take a risk! Take a chance! Goals are met and dreams are realized by risk takers, not by people who play it safe. You can't lose if you just take action!

JUST TAKE ACTION!

Suggested Exercises

- If you had three months to live—only three—and you knew for certain you would not live a day beyond that time, what would you do during those three months?

- Why aren't you doing those things now?

- Make a list of the things that you have been procrastinating about.

- Pick one thing on your list and take action toward accomplishing it.

KEEP ON GOING

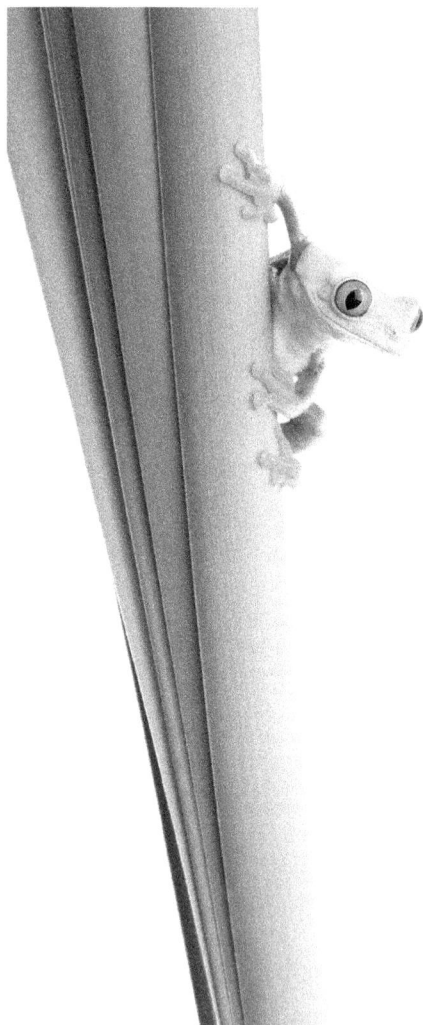

K

KEEP ON GOING

Sometimes we get tired. Sometimes life overwhelms us. We can't seem to get out of the pain caused by loss. Perhaps we lose a son in the Middle East conflict or a daughter to illness or a job or a marriage we thought would be lifelong.

How can we continue on the journey toward our goals when we are so overwhelmed? How can we continue when we are in so much pain?

When a situation looks hopeless, keep hoping. Don't quit. Keep going. When everything looks impossible, refuse to accept defeat. Don't quit. Keep going. People who succeed in the face of seemingly impossible conditions are people who don't know how to quit. What can we do when unexpected changes wreak havoc with our dreams? Avoid dwelling on loss. If you do, you will be discouraged and defeated. Instead of thinking about loss, concentrate on what you have left.

I want to share a story with you about refusing to quit. Walter Greving, a handsome northwest Iowan, suffered a severe bout of polio. When the disease left him, he took stock of the permanent damage. Chest muscles were paralyzed. He would spend the rest of his life on an artificial respirator. Walter's arms, legs, hands and shoulders, were all permanently paralyzed. However, he could still see, think, hear and talk. He still had the use of a single, solitary finger. Instead of dwelling on what he lost he began to think, "What can I do with what I have left?" He wondered "What can I do with one finger?"

He thought, "I could push a button which opens up an almost unlimited assortment of possibilities. A button starts a tape recorder and enables him to dictate the encouraging letters he sends around the world. A tape recorder, a radio, a TV and a book page flipper all can be enjoyed by using just one finger. He is quoted as saying, "I was never happier before polio than I am today. I never really started to live until I got into the iron lung. I learned to think differently. I didn't quit. I didn't give up. I kept going."

When ever you feel like giving up or packing it in, think of Walter Greving and keep going!

KEEP ON GOING

Suggested Exercises

- If you haven't written your goals down on paper, do so now. In fact, write them down on a card and carry it with you so you can look at it every chance you get.

- If one of your goals is a material item, get a picture of it and place it somewhere you can see it often. Write down motivational sayings on several cards and place them in your home and work area. Look at them often.

- For each goal you want to achieve, write a paragraph about why you want to achieve them. Include the reasons of why you must and will achieve them.

- What are some of the things that you may need to do that you don't want to do in order to achieve these goals? Write them down.

- Review your list of goals. Ask yourself if you are committed to achieving these goals. Do you have the passion to do anything it takes to achieve them? If you do, what is one small thing that you will do immediately toward achieving one of your goals?

- Review your list of the things that you may need to do that you don't want to do in order to achieve your goals. Decide which one of these things you will do this week toward achieving one of your goals.

- To make sure that you follow through, tell someone *what and when you are going to do it.* Now you've got your momentum back!

LOVE

L

LOVE YOURSELF

This may be a strange concept for some. It may even seem self-indulgent. Before we reach any of our goals, we must feel worthy enough to receive them.

If we think "I'm too fat," or "I'll never amount to anything," or "I'm too old," or "I'm not good enough," we undermine our self-image. We fail to reach our goals. If we feel too fat, we can start a weight loss program. Worrying about our weight takes focus off our goals. If debt stops us you from doing what we want, then start a financial plan and focus on prosperity. If we feel too old or too young or we don't deserve what we want, then reaching our goal is impossible until we change our focus from the negative to the positive.

Yes, there are some things we cannot change. However, we can change our perception of ourselves. See the power and creativity instead of limitations. There is a saying, "Fake it 'til you make it". Start looking in the mirror in the morning and say, "I love you and accept you just the way you are. You are worthy to receive your goals and dreams." Fake it until you believe it. Start embodying the positive feelings of loving yourself.

Love yourself enough to set good boundaries. Say "no" to people who want to use you or your time. Limit your time with people who do not support your goals. Avoid abusive people. What are other boundaries? How do you use your time? Are you focused on goals or do you waste time doing things that hinder progress?

Loving ourselves, allows goals and dreams to flourish in direct proportion to the positive perception we have of ourselves. We are wonderful, powerful and creative. We are worthy of having goals and dreams fulfilled. We are born for success!

LOVE YOURSELF

Suggested Exercises

- Write down at least eight things that you can do to show how much you love yourself.

- Write yourself a love letter.

- For the next 14 days take several minutes each morning to look in the mirror and repeat, "I love you (your name), and accept you just as your are."

- Write down some of the specific reasons why you love yourself.

MEDITATE

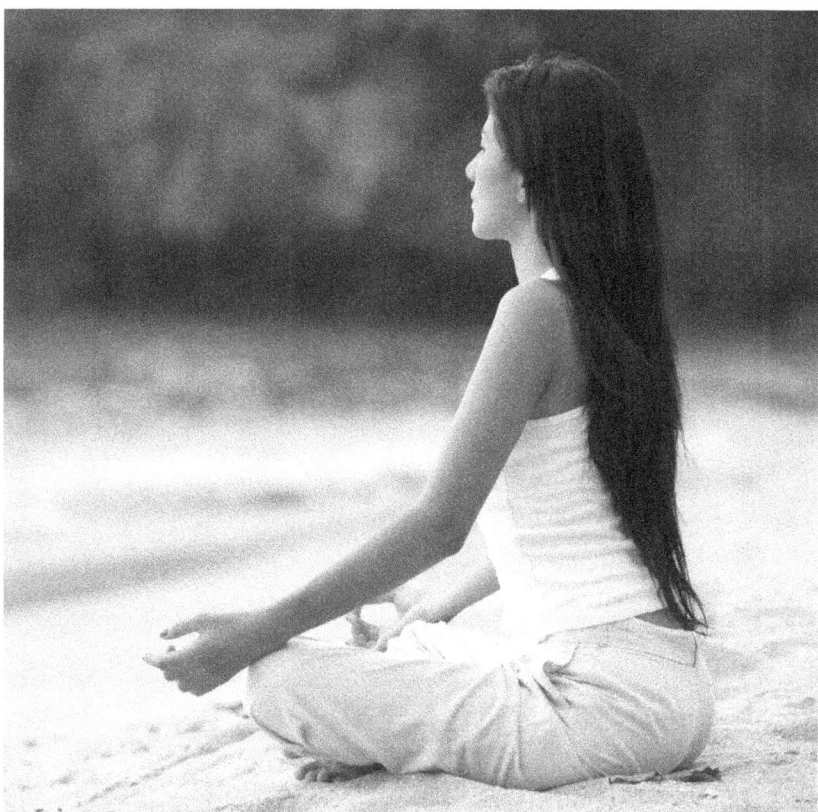

M

MEDITATE AND MAKE IT HAPPEN

Using the ABCs is a fun way of learning and acquiring the tools necessary to reach goals. Each letter holds a vital insight into life. "M" is one more letter that we can use to enrich our life. We can use "M" for meditating or making it happen, or both. Each has its own meaning, yet they work in concert with each other.

Meditating in the morning sets the tone for the day and helps us live in the moment. When we live life in the moment, we make life work. When we live in the now, we surrender and allow inspiration to be our motivation in achieving goals.

When we "make things happen" from our own will, i.e. your ego place, you may find the goals from that place are not fulfilling. Again, when we are open and allow ourselves to receive inspiration, life will offer us many riches.

Meditation helps us become aware of our higher selves, we start seeing our highest selves as a dimension of being which transcends the limitation of the physical world. Our highest selves have the capacity to attract all we need or desire.

Be one with your environment. See yourself as part of everyone and everything. Harness that power that makes things happen. Trust in the wisdom that created us, the wisdom that lives in our hearts and not our heads. Meditate on that wisdom and make it happen.

MAKE IT HAPPEN

Suggested Exercises

- Start meditating ten minutes each day for the next two weeks. If you haven't meditated before, light a candle and watch the flame flicker for those ten minutes.

- Write down your experience after each meditation.

- For the next two weeks meditate for 15 minutes each day. Try it without the candle.

- Continue to write down your experience after each meditation.

MEDITATION

Suggested Exercises

- Close your eyes, take in a deep breath in through your nose, hold it, and then slowly release it out of your mouth.

- Take another deep breath, hold it, and then slowly release it.

- Do this several more times and with each breath you take visualize yourself breathing in all the positive energy in the universe and when you slowly release it visualize yourself breathing out all the negative thoughts and feelings that you might be holding.

- Start relaxing your body by sending positive energy, first to your feet, then to you calves and then to your knees. Feel them letting go and relaxing. Now send that positive energy to your thighs, then to your abdomen and then to your arms and hands. Feel them letting go of any physical tightness and relaxing. Send positive energy to your heart. Feel your heart opening up and being ready to receive all the wonderful things that the universe has to offer you. Send positive energy to your neck, to your shoulders and finally to your head. Feel the muscles letting go in your neck and shoulders and in your head. Let the positive energy flow all through your body.

- Now visualize a beautiful light and watch this light as it gets larger and larger until it fills the entire inner vision of your mind. See within this beautiful light a special place of peace. It could be a temple or on a mountain or beach or park, or any other place you know is a safe place to share and to receive. Get comfortable in this safe place and invite God, as you understand God, or Spirit, or whoever you feel comfortable talking to. When they appear, share any concerns or problems you may have and ask for their advice. Hear what they have to tell you. Continue the dialog as long as it is comfortable for you. When you are done, thank them for coming and for the words they have spoken to you. Bid them goodbye and start leaving your safe place. See that beautiful golden light once again and watch it start to disappear. When you are ready come back to the room and open your eyes.

- Write down your experience.

NEVER LIE

N

NEVER LIE, CHEAT OR STEAL
ALWAYS STRIKE A FAIR DEAL

This letter represents one of the most powerful insights into how to create success. Lying, cheating, and stealing come from fear, not power. These qualities shouldn't represent who you are.

We have all come from that place at one time or another. If we are honest with ourselves, we acknowledge the difficulty in keeping a lie going. We put much energy into keeping our lies real. Lying is an energy waster.

Cheating someone does not stem from our highest consciousness. Cheating not only hurts the cheated; it hurts the cheater as well. Cheating diminishes integrity. Cheating produces an empty victory.

Stealing takes many forms. Stealing time from our job. Giving food away to your friends while working at a restaurant. Many people don't see either one as stealing. Everyone agrees about the obvious stealing of property or money. Stealing limits our ability to create what we want in our life.

Lying, cheating, and stealing are roadblocks on our journey. They keep us from reaching our destination.

Always play fair in business as well as our personal life. Integrity and honesty are our calling cards when dealing with others. When we act from our highest consciousness, we are in the most powerful creative place we can be, and our victories are glorious.

NEVER LIE, CHEAT OR STEAL
ALWAYS STRIKE A FAIR DEAL
Suggested exercises

• Reflect on your behavior of past jobs. Did you ever do personal business on an employer's time or talked excessively on personal phone calls? What other behavior did you have that might be interpreted as "stealing?" Write them down.

• Have you every taken something that wasn't yours from a person or a business? Reflect on the times that this behavior occurred. What was going on in your life at that time? Write down the behavior as well as what was going on in your life at that time.

• Have you had something taken from you? What? How did you feel? Write down what was taken and how that action made you feel.

• Since your level of integrity is really your "calling card," write down how you would like others to view you. What does your "calling card" say?

OPEN YOUR EYES

O

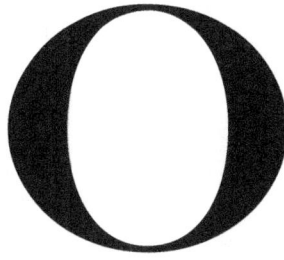

OPEN YOUR EYES AND SEE THINGS AS THEY REALLY ARE

Life is all about perception. How we perceive things is how we conceive things. Sometimes we are so busy focusing on the trivial, we do not see the forest for the trees. We go through life looking but not really seeing. We miss golden opportunities. We miss the chance to reach our goals. We miss opportunities for success.

There is so much to see if we really learn to look. Think about the last person you saw on the street you presumed to be homeless. His clothes may be tattered, he may need a bath or a shave. However, this is just the surface. What are the eyes of your heart seeing? Open them up and see this man as someone with a story to tell, lessons to teach and who needs love, just like you. See with your heart. See what is really there.

When I was a young girl my father served in the military. We moved several times due to his transfers. At one place, I spent many an afternoon sitting on the porch with a elderly man who shared stories from his youth. He was blind and told me he really did not see until he lost his sight. He was not born blind. It was amazing to hear how he saw life through the eyes of his heart. He told me that he had taken his sight for granted. His words have guided me through my life. He taught me to look at a tree, take time to see the bark, look carefully at all the life that moves in and around that bark. When looking at the leaves, look closely at the veins. See how they make an intricate design within the leaf. See how they attach to the branches; see how the branches weave in and around the tree like a beautiful piece of art.

Take time to look closely at someone. Notice their eyes, their smile and their expression. These are the windows into who they really are and what they are feeling. The windows let you in to someone's heart.

As a young girl, this blind elderly man really touched my heart. Since then I try to see with my heart. So, I pass his words to you. Open your eyes and see things as they really are. Appreciate everyone and everything in nature as a piece of art. Your success will be your creative masterpiece.

OPEN YOUR EYES

Suggested Exercises

- This week take a walk through a forest, a park, or hike on a nature trail. Take note of what you see. Are there trees? Flowers? Birds? Ground squirrels? What do you see? Pay attention to all the details of each thing you see. Write them down. Oh, and by the way, leave your cell phone at home!

- When meeting someone new, pretend you have to introduce this person to someone without describing his or her obvious physical features. How would you go about doing that? Where would you start? Maybe start with looking into their eyes and listening to what your heart is telling you.

- Make a list of all the things that you focus on that really don't matter. Review this list and see how they are blocking your real vision.

- Have you missed any opportunities in your life because your focus was on one of those things that really didn't matter? If so, write those missed opportunities down. Review the list and decide to focus on your goals and dreams instead.

PRACTICE

P

PRACTICE MAKES PERFECT

Whatever your personal goal, or dream, whatever riches in life you want to embrace; practice, practice, practice. It takes practice to accomplish goals.

Practice takes work. I took piano lessons when I was a young girl and performed in recitals. I hated to practice. However, I knew I wouldn't know how to play the song if I didn't practice, and I would be embarrassed. So I practiced, practiced and practiced.

"Practice makes Perfect" is a saying denoting "work." However without practice, living a full life just doesn't happen.

The famous fliers known as the Thunderbirds perform at air shows with maneuvers that form art in the sky. They practice flying every day. Many maneuvers are very hard on their bodies. However, their goal is to perform as a squadron and be the very best. That is their goal, their dream. So, they practice, practice, practice.

Another kind of practice is practicing presence. Being in the now. The secret of harmonious living or manifesting a rich full life is living in the now; this moment. We must develop a spiritual consciousness of the now. A consciousness free from fear, anxiety, anger, jealousy, gossip and judgment. When we judge, gossip, or come from any other feelings described earlier, we don't live in the present. We either live in the past or wonder about the future. It takes practice to develop spiritual consciousness and live in the moment.

To live in our highest consciousness takes practice. Reaching goals or living life more fully may seem to demand greater strength, knowledge, and abilities. There may be greater financial demands than we can meet. Keep focused on what you want. Avoid the "I can't" trap. We can do anything we put our minds to.

Practice living in the moment. Develop the consciousness to support your dreams. Practice holding the highest quality of thoughts. We must rid ourselves of anger, judgment, and fear. Remember your dreams! Embrace a higher level of consciousness to start living in the now. Eckart Tolle tells us, when we come from anger, or we can't forgive someone, or we can't accept others as they are, we are not living in the present. So, each time we are upset, or are tempted to judge another person, stop, and ask yourself, "Am I coming from my highest place right now?" If your answer is "no," start developing a higher consciousness. Experience the harmony that comes from living in the present. So, practice, practice, practice.

PRACTICE MAKES PERFECT
Suggested Exercises

- Living in the present moment is sometimes very difficult. Practice living in the moment with these suggested exercises.

- When listening to music, pay attention to the words, rhythm and sentiments.

- This week, when taking a shower, be very mindful of the water coming out of the showerhead. Feel every drop of water that hits your body. Inhale and exhale slowly while feeling the water coming down on you. When finished, give thanks for the opportunity to experience the water in such a mindful way.

- This week, when taking care of basic chores around your house—doing the dishes, cleaning or washing clothes—consider each chore the most important thing in life. Treat each chore as a sacred action. When finished, give thanks for the opportunity to experience these tasks.

- Get a piece of paper and a pencil. Set a timer for ten minutes. Sit quietly and focus only on positive thoughts. Every time a negative thought comes into your mind make a little mark on your paper. If you judge yourself for thinking that negative thought make another mark on the paper. At the end of the ten minutes count up the marks on your paper. How many marks did you have? Multiply that number by six and that is how many negative thoughts you have in an hour. You can continue to multiply the hours by the day, week, month and year if you want. However, the point of this exercise is to make you aware of your negative thinking.

- This week pay attention to any negative thoughts that come into your mind. At that moment, ask it to leave or replace it with a positive one. Continue this exercise each day until it becomes a habit of eliminating your negative thinking or replacing it with a positive thought.

- If your goal requires learning a new skill, practice working on that new skill every day for the next 30 days.

QUITTERS NEVER WIN

Q

QUITTERS NEVER WIN AND WINNERS NEVER QUIT

Every time we feel like giving up on our goals and forgetting our dreams and quit, think of all the people who influence our lives in such wonderful and positive ways because they didn't quit. They may have experienced many a trial and tribulation in reaching their goals.

Orville and Wilbur Wright never gave up, even though they endured many years of research, disappointments, and disasters before their first model flying machine flew more than five minutes. That was in 1904 and was the beginning of aviation. No one would have blamed them if they had given up and quit. They didn't and because they didn't we have air travel today. They were winners.

Summertime in the 1950s was a time of fear and anxiety for many parents when children by the thousands became infected with crippling polio. Through many painstaking years of research, Dr. Jonas Salk discovered a vaccine. He didn't quit searching. He was a winner and so were the children saved by his vaccine.

Think about Alexander Graham Bell, the father of telecommunications or Dr. Martin Luther King, Jr. and the civil rights movement. Then go back to striving toward your goal. If you don't quit, it is a win-win for everyone. If your dreams come true, you may contribute to society in some wonderful way, too.

Think about someone you respect and admire for his or her tenacity. Someone who didn't quit. Someone who kept going until they reached their goals and saw their dreams come true. Use them as your mentor—and remember, "Quitters don't win and winners don't quit."

QUITTERS NEVER WIN AND WINNERS NEVER QUIT

Suggested Exercises

- Research people who were or who are famous. Review their stories until you find someone who had many seemingly impossible obstacles to overcome— someone who never quit going toward his or her goal. Write at least one paragraph about the qualities that they possessed that kept them going.

- Review your writing and use it as a motivator anytime you feel like quitting.

- List the qualities you have that will keep you from quitting.

- Review your list and use it as a motivator toward becoming a winner.

READ

R

READ, STUDY, AND LEARN WHAT IS IMPORTANT IN YOUR LIFE

Embrace and appreciate acquired knowledge. Take classes, go to seminars, join study groups. Study and learn from anyone that helps you on your journey to fulfilling your dreams.

Give yourself permission to read books any way you want. Peruse, skip around, read the chapters you want. Reading is more enjoyable that way and learning can be more fun.

When we are in school or learning a new job, we need to read and learn just to pass or graduate or do the job. However, when we read or learn about our passion and what makes our hearts sing, reading and learning takes on a whole new meaning.

For example, if one of your goals is to learn more about religion, then we may want to read inspirational writings from other cultures, religions, and philosophies. Sutras, are words set in prose, that speak to Buddhists. The Upanishads in Hinduism are also prose texts as well as dialogues. The Tao Te Ching, the written principle of Taoism meaning the Way and the Virtue, written like a prayer book and speaks about the Tao, the way, the force, an energy, a power. In Christianity there is the New Testament where we find the gospels speaking about the teachings of Jesus. All these writings and more teach us about religious belief systems.

If our goal is to fly a plane, we can read read and learn about the mechanics of the plane in addition to taking flying lessons. If a goal is opening a restaurant, we can read about management as well as cuisine. We can learn the meaning of mythology. Reading books written by experts in that field not only teaches us about mythological stories and symbols, we learn about life.

These are all examples, of course. Whatever our goals, read, study, and learn.

READ, STUDY, AND LEARN WHAT IS IMPORTANT IN YOUR LIFE

Suggested Exercises

- Write down how you spend your time. Next to each item write down how much time you spend doing it.

- Review your list. Are you spending too much time on things that will not assist you in achieving your goals?

- What are you currently reading? Are you reading books, articles or journals that will help you acquire the knowledge you need to achieve your goals?

- What have you learned new in the last month? Will this knowledge help you in achieving your goals?

- Are you taking any classes or going to seminars that will assist you in achieving your goals?

- For the next week spend less time on the things that will not assist you in achieving your goals and more time on reading or studying material that will assist you.

- Do you know anyone who has already accomplished or achieved some of the same goals and dreams you aspire to? If possible, talk to them and learn from them.

STOP
PROCRASTINATING

S

STOP PROCRASTINATING

Procrastination is a habit we must break so dreams may come true.

We procrastinate for many reasons. We procrastinate because we fear failure. We procrastinate because we feel unworthy of fulfillment. It really doesn't matter why we procrastinate, we need to stop. Our success depends on it.

Take action! Any action is better than inaction. What are you putting off that needs doing to get what you want? Is it something you don't like to do or something you think takes too long to do? Is it something you feel embarrassed about? It really doesn't matter why. Action is the only cure.

Procrastination keeps us from that new job, or new relationship, or making enough money to buy a new house or new car. So stop right now! Think of three tasks to help you get going. Even small tasks help, like writing that long overdue letter, or folding laundry. Write down three small tasks down after reading this chapter. Pick one of them to do before going on to the next letter.

If we procrastinate about writing down and choosing one small task to do right now, think about what procrastination costs us in the big picture. Remember, we cannot walk the path to reach our goals with our feet in buckets of cement. Those buckets represent procrastination. Chip away at the cement, free your feet, and get moving!

STOP PROCRASTINATING

Suggested Exercises

- What are three simple things you could do that you have been putting off? Write them down.

- Pick one thing and do it today.

- Reward yourself.

- List two new actions you could take to assist you in achieving your goals.

- Pick one of these actions and accomplish it within the next week.

- Reward yourself.

- Review your goals. Get excited about them. See yourself already achieving them. Take the second action and you'll be on your way to success!

TAKE CONTROL OF YOUR DESTINY

We have the power within us to attract all that we could ever want to ourselves. This power is not based on belief; it is a *knowing*. This miraculous power goes untapped primarily because of our conditioning. We must take control of our own destiny by cultivating this knowing and avoiding clutter, like preconceptions, blocking our path.

Take control by becoming aware of your higher self. Dreams come true for people who see the invisible. People who see the invisible do what others call impossible. The invisible is the potential inside all of our bones, arteries, and skin.

We ask ourselves what causes the giant oak tree to become what it is. It progresses from a tiny acorn to a seedling that grows into a mighty tree. Our logical, rational mind suggest, there must be something resembling "treeness," within that acorn. When we open an acorn, we find nothing resembling a tree. All we will find is a mass of brown stuff, like dust. Looked at more closely, this dust would reveal molecules, then atoms, then subatomic particles, until we find waves of energy coming and going mysteriously. That is the invisible potential in all of us.

We become aware of our potential by seeing ourselves as a dimension transcending the limitations of the physical world like that acorn.

Once we know we are more than just blood, skin and bones, we can see full potential. It starts growing like the mighty oak tree. We attract what we desire to ourselves. Our ideas come from our highest place, where the invisible become visible. The place that attracts energy to grow your potential.

Controlling our destiny means taking full responsibility for our lives. Blame no one, including yourself, for any setbacks. We must examine attitudes we hold about life. Rearrange any inner perceptions that don't support who we really are.

You are someone who is still growing into your potential. We are more than flesh and bone. We have the same energy inside us as that acorn.

If we control our own destiny, we will reach our goals and experience our full potential. Success!

TAKE CONTROL OF YOUR DESTINY

Suggested Exercises

- What small successes did you have yesterday that you are thankful for? Write them down.

- Make a renewed commitment today towards your goals. Write that commitment down.

- Write down what kind of legacy you want to leave.

- Create a worksheet to see how you are balancing the roles and activities of your life. Include work, personal, family, friends, community and your goals. Under personal, list how you are taking care of yourself. Under family, list how you are connecting and spending time with your loved ones and do the same with friends. Under work, list how much time you spend at your job or career and under community, list your involvement in organizations and activities. Under the heading of "your goals," list how much time you are spending on what it takes to achieve them.

- Review your worksheet. Examine how you have scheduled yourself into these different areas of your life. If you think there is an imbalance, write down how you want to reschedule yourself into these different areas and make the changes necessary to get your life back into balance.

UNDERSTAND YOURSELF

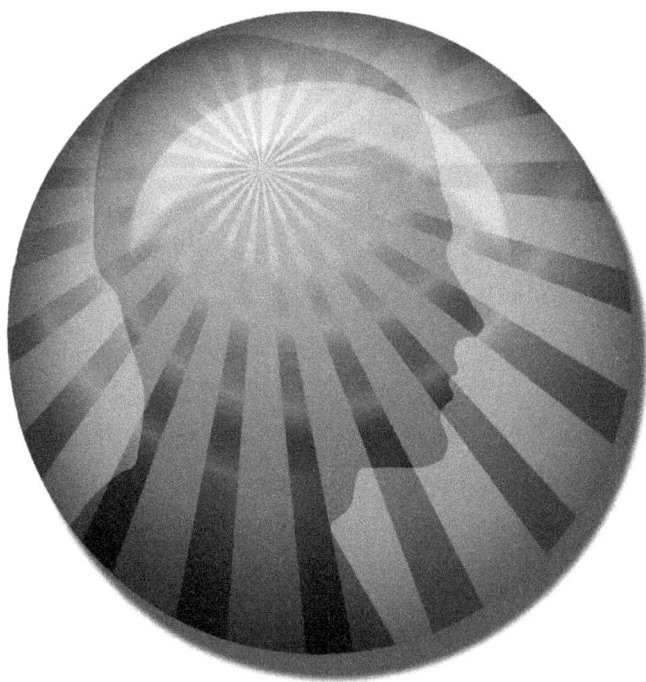

U

UNDERSTAND YOURSELF TO BETTER UNDERSTAND OTHERS

Human beings have the ability to think as well as feel. We must understand and *feel* feelings, not just *think* about feeling. When someone asks how you feel about a certain situation, do you answer with your heart or your head? So many times we answer with our head, expressing our feelings in an intellectual way. We are not really aware of how we do feel because we lack understanding of ourselves. Become aware of your "feeling bank". Know yourself more intimately. What makes you happy, sad, glad, melancholy, joyous, or grateful?

Before others can understand us, we must understand ourselves. If we don't, opportunities may pass us by, because we will not recognize them. You will be happy when you reach your goal; however, you will be on your journey until you do so. We meet many people on our way offering us advice to shorten our journey and bring success closer. Unless we really understand what makes our hearts sing, we may not recognize opportunities, miss out on something great.

Trying to understand others is another component to "U." Try to understand someone's point of view, rather than getting them to see yours. Listen to what they really say, not just with their words but also with their hearts. Relationships will be more harmonious and rich.

UNDERSTAND YOURSELF TO
BETTER UNDERSTAND OTHERS

Suggested Exercises

• To help you understand yourself a little better, write down the following:

"I cry when   "

"I feel sad when   "

"I feel frustrated when   "

"I feel resentful when   "

"My heart sings when   "

"I feel impatient when   '

"I feel guilt when   "

"I feel ashamed when   "

"I feel afraid when   "

• Review your list and add ten more "I" feeling statements. Here are some sample keywords:

Adventurous	Agitated	Hurt
Affectionate	Angry	Bored
Alive	Helpless	Relieved
Appreciative	Fearful	Satisfied
Blissful	Exhausted	Annoyed
Cheerful	Mean	Stimulated
Complacent	Jealous	Joyful
Inspired	Worried	Proud
Confident	Suspicious	
Joyful	Lonely	
Peaceful	Irritated	

- Think of someone you think you know well. Do the same exercise for them. How would they fill in the blanks in exercise one? See if you can do the second exercise as well. What ten feeling words would they choose and how would they fill in those blanks?

- After completing the above exercises take time to reflect on how you felt doing them and journal your feelings.

VISUALIZE

V

VISUALIZE WHAT YOU WANT

After 11 long years and many obstacles, my daughter Julie, graduated from a master's program in Speech Language Pathology. She never lost sight of her goal, even though her journey was long with many roadblocks to overcome. Julie imagined herself doing what she wanted to do. Then she created a mental picture of what that looked like, and set off on her journey. She started at a community college in her hometown. Then she moved to another city to attend a second community college with the goal of attending a four-year university in that same city. Julie worked in a bank, then at a food mart, to pay for her schooling. She was rejected twice by that university. She continued taking courses at the local community college hoping she would get into the university the next semester. That did not happen. Julie packed up her bags, moved back to her hometown and attended a university from which she graduated. Though it took Julie 11 years to complete the journey, she created a mental picture and never lost sight of it.

Have a fixed goal, a clear picture of your desire and don't become confused or frustrated by negativity from others. Counteract them by thinking and radiating positive thoughts.

Create a mental picture. Believe it will materialize with all your heart. We hear over and over again, "Believe you can do it and you can." "It is done unto you as you believe." Imagination, visualization, creating a mental picture and believing leads to accomplishment. Belief enables a person to do what others think is impossible.

Our behavior results from thoughts that precede it. If we visualize ourselves as incompetent, we create incompetence. A thought is the first step in the process of visualization. Our entire life experience revolves around the image of ourselves. Virtually everything we do is a result of the picture we place in our minds before we make the attempt.

Once we create our mental picture, we begin converting it into reality. Remember what Albert Einstein taught us about time. Time does not exist in the linear world. Time is humankind's invention due to our limited vision and need to compartmentalize everything. There really is no such thing as time. Everything you are capable of visualizing already exists.

We cannot visualize something, then sit around and wait for it to materialize. The opportunity for bringing thought to physical reality is up to us. We must be willing to do whatever it takes to make our mental pictures a reality. This is the single most important aspect of visualization. Remember, there is no failure. There are only results. Our concept of failure comes from believing someone else's opinion about how we could do something differently

So, dream, dream, dream—visualize your dream. Tell yourself it is already here. Be willing to do whatever is necessary to create a reality from visualization. Realize there is no such thing as failure, only results. We journey towards our dream step by step. Remember, "It is done unto you as you *believe*." Success is just one step away!

VISUALIZE WHAT YOU WANT

Suggested Exercises

- If you haven't done a "vision or dream board" I suggest you do one now. Get a poster board and plenty of magazines, a pair of scissors, some glue, markers, crayons, paints and any other creative aides you might like to use and start creating. Using pictures from magazines or ones that you have drawn, create a collage of your vision.

- When you have finished your project put it where you can see it every day.

- Every time you make a new goal, create another vision board, or add it to your existing one.

WANT IT

WANT IT MORE THAN ANYTHING

Your success depends on the amount of passion you wrap around your goals. Passion is the motivating force driving us all. When we want something so bad we can taste it, smell it and feel it, we create it. The time it takes us to reach a goal depends on the degree of passion we feel. Want it more than anything!

Many years ago I invited some Navajo women and their families to join us for the holidays. I didn't realize most of them had never been off their northern Arizona reservation, let alone make the 900-mile drive to California. When they told me someone would loan them a camper pickup truck for all 11 of them, I knew right then and there they might not make it. I really wanted them to join us for the holidays, since they were so gracious to my family the year before. I wanted to show the same hospitality to them.

My friends and I put our heads together. All I could think about was getting my friends here with their families. All of sudden an acquaintance approached me at a function and asked if I were comfortable driving a big 15-passenger van. I said "Sure." But I really didn't know if I could. Her husband worked for a car dealership and arranged for a brand new, never driven, 15-passenger van.

To shorten a very long story, I drove the huge van, ran into a blizzard, slid on ice, almost got stuck in mud on the reservation's dirt roads, but I arrived. My passion, desire, and wanting to get there more than anything got me there. I brought back four women and 11 children. With the help of my friends, I arranged gifts for all the children to be under the tree when we arrived back home. My family and I had the best Christmas ever.

Nothing is possible without passion. I wanted this more than anything. It was validation that you can have whatever you want, if you want it more than anything!

WANT IT MORE THAN ANYTHING

Suggested Exercises

- Think about the times in your life where passion played a part in achieving what it was you set out to get or accomplish. Make a list of those times.

- Review your list and put yourself back into those times. Close your eyes and feel what that passion felt like. What did it feel like when you got what you wanted or when you accomplished what you set out to do? Bring that feeling to the goals and dreams you presently have.

- Hold that passion and renew the excitement about your goals and dreams. Write a paragraph about the passion you currently hold toward your goals and dreams. Read and reread this paragraph over and over and over until that passion becomes part of you.

XCELLERATE

X

XCELLERATE YOUR EFFORTS

You're almost there. Just a little more to go! Don't slack off as you get closer to goals. Don't slow down thinking you have it made. Keep up the momentum!

Marathon runners start off slowly in the beginning of their race and increase their speed as the race goes on. However, as they close in on the finish line, they use their last bit of energy thrusting forward to break that ribbon for the win. So as you close in on your finish line, increase your efforts to reach your goal. Success is our Golden Cup; our Blue Ribbon.

We use the tools we acquire along the way to help us Xcellerate our efforts. Spend more time on whatever needs doing. Give up one hour of television or get up an hour earlier. Do whatever it takes to propel you to the finish line. Go back and read these ABCs. Use "E" representing excitement. Get excited about almost being there. Remember "J"—Just take action!

We're close to the last letter of our ABCs. Success is just around the corner.

XCELLERATE YOUR EFFORTS

Suggested Exercises

- Today or tomorrow, where could you find an extra hour to work on your goals? Write down where you could find an extra hour every day this week. Maybe watch television an hour less or get up an hour earlier.

- Take these extra hours and spend them working toward your goals. Write down some action steps you could take. Then take them.

YESTERDAY
IS GONE

Y

YESTERDAY IS GONE, TOMORROW MAY NOT COME, TODAY IS ALL YOU HAVE

Don't live in the past! We all hear the saying "Don't cry over spilled milk." The past is over. The check is cashed. Let go of whatever has happened in the past. It holds us back from continuing on our journey to success. You are the author of your life. Write a new chapter. You cannot rewrite the past.

Avoid living in the future too! The future may not look the way you think it will. Another popular saying is "The check is in the mail." You don't have that check in your hand and you may never get it.

Today is all you have. The present. Now. You received the check, cashed it and the money is in your hand. Avoid wasting today by reliving the past or day-dreaming about future success. Make a call or write that overdue letter. Or think big by writing a business plan or finishing an overdue project.

Success depends on what we do today. The actions we take today help us write the next chapter of our lives. We cannot relive our past. Yesterday is gone. Tomorrow may not come. Day-dreaming about the future without action is a waste of precious time. Time we could spend doing something to make our dreams a reality.

You are the author of your life. Start writing your next chapter today. Live in the present.

YESTERDAY IS GONE, TOMORROW MAY NOT COME, TODAY IS ALL YOU HAVE

Suggested Exercises

- If you find yourself trying to relive the past or daydreaming about the future, do something different than your normal routine right away. This will help you change your thought patterns. Changing your thought patterns will interrupt your obsessing about the past or daydreaming about the future. What are some things that you could do differently today? Write them down and for the next week and practice doing them.

ZERO IN

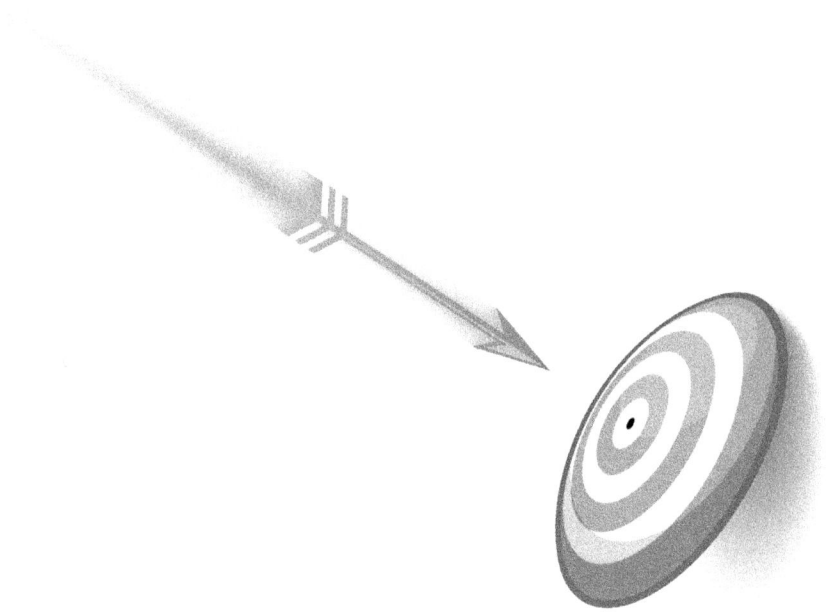

Z

ZERO IN ON YOUR TARGET— AND GO FOR IT!

This is the last letter in our ABCs to your success series.

There are times we have a target, a goal or a dream that does not come to pass? Why didn't I reach it? Why did I stop short just as I was getting close? Was I afraid? Did I lack commitment? If the answer was "yes" to any of these questions, take a good look at which "why" stopped you.

Zeroing in on a target requires commitment, certainty and willingness.

Commitment is an intention and not just an idea. Stopping short translates into lack of commitment. Ask yourself, "Is this really what I want in life?" Are you committed to your goal really? Are you willing to do what it takes to stay committed to it? Remember, commitment means change. Are you ready for change? Are you fearful to make changes brought about by reaching your target? Is there a difference between interest and commitment? There is a big difference. "I really would like to make more money." "I would like to have my own home." "I would really like to make a difference in the world." "I would like..." These statements are not commitments at all. They are statements of a preference. They say, "I'm interested in having this happen if I don't have to do anything." This does not come from the powerful place inside us. It comes from a weak plea made without the energy to launch it.

One day in 1955 a young black woman stepped onto a bus in Montgomery, Alabama. She refused to give up her seat to a white person as she was legally required. That moment was the beginning of the civil rights movement. Was Rosa Parks thinking of the future when she refused to relinquish her seat on that bus? Did she have a divine plan for how she could change the structure of society? Perhaps. Her commitment to hold herself to a higher standard compelled her to act. What a far-reaching effect one woman's commitment has made by not giving up her seat.

If we have clear convictions and a strong spiritual or religious path, we can hold tight to our goal and keep zeroed in on the target. We can rid ourselves of the fear that blocks us from doing so. By staying on our chosen spiritual path, trusting in a Power greater than ourselves will get us out of our own way. Commit to a goal, state it as an intention, zero in on the target, and allow the Power inside to take over.

Make the decision to commit to your dream. Walk your chosen path with conviction. Commit to your goal and you will hit the bull's-eye. Zero in and go for it!

ZERO IN ON YOUR TARGET— AND GO FOR IT!

Suggested Exercises

- Draw a target and put your goal or dream in the bull's-eye. Draw arrows in the different rings indicating where you are in reaching them.

- Each time you take some action toward your goal move or add an arrow to the next ring closer to the bull's-eye.

- Now write your commitment and intention on a piece of paper and place it next to your goal in the bull's-eye.

- When your arrow hits the bull's-eye—celebrate!

BIBLIOGRAPHY

Bristol, Claude M. (1985)
The Magic of Believing, The Science of Setting Your Goal and Then Reaching It.
Prentice Hall, New York, NY

Brussat, Frederic and Mary Ann (1996)
Spiritual Literacy, Reading the Sacred in Everyday Life. Simon and Schuster,
New York, NY

Brussat, Frederic and Mary Ann (2000)
Spiritual Rx, Prescriptions for Living a Meaningful Life. Hyperion, NY

Butterworth, Eric (1983)
Spiritual Economics, the Prosperity Process. Unity School of Christianity,
Unity Village, MO

Canfield, Jack and Mark Victor Hanson (1994)
Dare to Win. Berkley, New York, NY

Chopra, Deepak (1994)
*The Seven Spiritual Laws of Success, a Practical Guide to the Fulfillment
of your Dreams.* Co-published by Amber–Allen and New World Library,
San Rafael, CA

Covey, Stephen R. (1989)
The 7 Habits of Highly Effective People, Powerful Lessons in Personal Change.
Simon & Schuster, Inc., New York, NY

Cole-Whitaker, Terry (1979)
What You Think of Me is None of My Business. A.S. Barnes and Co., Inc.,
San Diego, CA

Dyer, Dr. Wayne (1992)
Real Magic, Creating Miracles in Everyday Life. Harper Collins Publishers, Inc.,
New York, NY

Dyer, Dr. Wayne (1997)
*Manifest Your Destiny, The Nine Spiritual Principles for Getting Everything
You Want.* Harper Collins Publishers, Inc., New York, NY

Dyer, Dr. Wayne (2004)
The Power of Intention, Learning to Co-create Your World Your Way.
Hay House, Inc. Carlsbad, CA

Hanh, Thich Nhat (1975)
The Miracle of Mindfulness, A Manual on Meditation.
Beacon Press, Boston, MA

Patent, Arnold M. (1991)
You Can Have it All. Celebration Publishing, Sylva, NC

Robbins, Anthony (1993)
Awaken the Giant Within: How to Take Immediate Control of Your Mental, Emotional, Physical and Financial Destiny. Simon & Schuster, New York, NY

Roger, John and Peter McWilliams (1988)
You Can't Afford the Luxury of a Negative Thought. Prelude Press, Los Angeles, CA

Tolle, Eckhart (1999)
The Power of Now, A Guide to Spiritual Enlightenment. New World Library, Novato, CA

www.ingramcontent.com/pod-product-compliance
Lightning Source LLC
Chambersburg PA
CBHW031323040426

42443CB00005B/198